Writing Examples

By

Kisali Wijesekara

MAPLE
PUBLISHERS

Writing Examples

Author: Kisali Wijesekara

Copyright © Kisali Wijesekara (2023)

The right of Kisali Wijesekara to be identified as author of this work has been asserted by the author in accordance with section 77 and 78 of the Copyright, Designs and Patents Act 1988.

First Published in 2023

ISBN 978-1-915796-40-0 (Paperback)

Cover Design by: Kisali Wijesekara

Book Layout by:
   Maple Publishers
   www.maplepublishers.com

Published by:
   Maple Publishers
   Fairbourne Drive, Atterbury,
   Milton Keynes,
   MK10 9RG, UK
   www.maplepublishers.com

A CIP catalogue record for this title is available from the British Library.

All rights reserved. No part of this book may be reproduced or translated by any form or by any means, electronic or mechanical, including photocopying, recording or by any information storage and retrieval system without written permission from the author.

The views expressed in this work are solely those of the author and do not reflect the opinions of Publishers, and the Publisher hereby disclaims any responsibility for them.

This book is written, typed and illustrated by Kisali Wijesekara.

Hi, I am Kisali, and I have just turned 12, but I wrote most of these pieces when I was 9 and 10 years old.

When I was younger, reading other children's writing really inspired me to get better at my writing and I'd always magpie bits and bobs to improve my own writing. So I decided to make this book to help other children improve their writing too. I gradually got better at writing over the years thanks to the help I received from Mrs Sarah Taylor and my year 4/5 teacher, Miss Kwakye.

I have many hobbies, but art is one of my favourite ones.

(An example of my artwork)

Contents

Story Writing	5
Description	29
News Report	37
Report	45
Diaries	49
Letters	55
Leaflets	67
Argument	75
Articles	79
Fact file	81
Script	83
Glossary	87

Writing Examples

Story Writing

My tips:

- When writing a story, use POS AM to remember to use personification, onomatopoeia, similes, alliteration and metaphors.

- Use as much advanced vocabulary as possible.

- Use indirect and direct speech.

- Stick to informal language.

- Use a variety of punctuation, such as ellipsis and colons.

- You can always reuse phrases that you've used before.

- Remember you can use alliteration in your title.

Kisali Wijesekara

Song Snatcher Steals Sophie's Song!

The scintillating sunshine was soaring in the azure-blue sky, while the gentle breeze played with me. Leaves were zooming around like race cars, flowers dancing and the trees were whispering. There I was, sitting on the bench after running around like a lunatic. After all, I was at the park. Out of the blue, I spotted a diary under the bench. Who on Earth could it belong to?

I was so eager to open it! I was far too inquisitive for a 12-year-old girl. My curiosity did eventually get control of me, and I opened it…

"7/8/2021

Dear diary,

You'll never guess what happened today! The song I stole from Sophie-Rose earned me millions. I'm exhilarated! However, what shall I do with the pathetic girl? She nearly escaped from her cell. If she ever succeeds, I'm dead! She won't. Anyway, I'm world famous now! Yay! – Juliet V."

I was furious and my face turned as red as a tomato. I admired Juliet's songs and to know she stole it from someone else… I was devastated! I was in a state of disbelief. My idol was a CRIMINAL! Even as a child, I knew that this was copyright and against the law. Therefore, I phoned the police. I felt betrayed!

Suddenly, I heard someone run towards me, frightened. I hid in the shrubbery. Juliet! "Thank goodness nobody found it! I was about to go crazy," she panted, relieved. The police had arrived. BANG! It sounded like a gunshot. I peered from the bushes to see Juliet's hand raised in the air. They took her diary. "This is ridiculous. Utterly ridiculous!" she roared like a lion.

The officer read through her diary and commanded, "Take her to the station and send a search party to her basement." I had saved the day, plus I had also learned never to write anything unimportant or rude in my diary!

Emily's Excellent Escape!

As the ominous grey clouds crept across the sky, the mischievous mice scuttled around on the icy floor (made of pure ice). The frozen Kingdom. Home to a devious and wicked fiend, known as the Ice Queen, who had skin as pale as a ghost and long static hair as white as snow. A sinister smirk lay on her face as she kept a young, innocent, and humble girl, Emily, hostage in a cell which gradually drained her of energy. Emily had long, lovely hair that was as red as lava; it shot up bursting with life.

BANG! BANG! Someone other than the Ice Queen had entered the room. Emily was exhilarated. Thrilled! "You!" snapped the odd looking man, "Where is the Ice Queen?"

"I-I don't kn..." muttered Emily, as she was rudely interrupted.

"Don't you dare lie to me, peasant!" the mysterious man commanded. Bing! Emily came up with a cunning plan. She was going to trick him. So, she began...

Emily was free. She succeeded in fooling him into unlocking the cell. She had told him that the throne (which was covered by an intricate design) was concealed behind the solid stone wall with the Ice Queen residing in it. The floor began shaking violently, as if an earthquake had occurred. Candles flickered. "Now the ice monster will come to you!" Emily stated, as she vanished through the shadows.

The Ice Queen arrived red-faced. "What. Did. You. Do!" screamed the omnipotent Ice Queen as she towered above the man mercilessly, whilst her beady eyes scanned the room for clues on what had happened. She darts her head back at him in realisation, "I'll deal with you later. That pesky rat is trying to escape," the Ice Queen bellowed as she began to bark orders at her trustworthy guards.

Emily on the other hand, found Scruffy – an enormous eagle -after incessantly stumbling over the blanket of snow. She was over the moon as she hopped onto Scruffy's back and soared into the sky. Suddenly, web-like traps began raining down as the wind whistled. The Ice Queen stood holding her staff, which let out an eerie green glow. Emily could feel her blood boil. Hastily, she tilted her head forwards. Her heart was pounding. Her spine was tingling. Her eyes widened in complete horror.

"SSSCCRUUFFFYY!" Emily screamed at the top of her lungs as she fixated her eyes on the incoming web. What was going to happen?

The Mysterious Locked Door!

Beatrice was an inquisitive girl for her age – she was only twelve. The curious mind she had, had almost always taken control of her (which caused her to get in trouble regularly). Beautiful Beatrice had smooth, soft and silky blonde hair which nearly reached her hips. With aqua-blue eyes, that twinkle in the sunlight.

It had been approximately two weeks after moving house. The new house was dull, bleak, and gloomy in Beatrice's opinion. Especially her room: what was rather peculiar was the double-sided key, which clung to a silver chain that she discovered in a small wooden box. That day onwards, it always dangled from Beatrice's neck.

Recently, she had been peering at what looked like a door, which had a miniature handle. Beatrice yanked on it with all her might, so that her pale cheeks became tomatoes, but it still didn't budge the slightest bit! Suddenly, the key around her neck began to tickle her chest. This took her mind off the door for a split second.

"Oh!" she exclaimed, realizing she had a key. The key fit on her first try. It was as easy as using a knife to slice through butter. Creeeaeaeck... The door opened, revealing a sizeable room which was pitch-black! It was as dark as the midnight sky. The deafening silence was disturbed by my footsteps which caused the floorboards to squeak. Beatrice cautiously walked in...

BANG! The door slammed shut with such ferocity that it sent a wave of wind, which whipped Beatrice's ice-cold cheeks. Beatrice was scared of one thing only: the dark. "AGH!" screamed Beatrice. However, no one heard. The key, Beatrice thought. Her thoughts were racing. Her heart was pounding. It was spine tingling.

Immediately, she flipped the copper key and carefully placed it in the keyhole. She was never grateful to catch a glimpse of sunlight, but at this very moment, she was.

As fast as lightning she bolted down the flight of stairs. In the end she learned her lesson, don't explore things you weren't meant to.

The Horrifying Haunted House

It was almost noon when the angry clouds began to cry miserably and at this point a hazy mist dropped, too. The atmosphere was dull and gloomy when Harriet found herself lost and drenched in the downpour. She was accompanied by her beautiful, beloved dog – Sky. One thing in common between the two was their petite appearance. Harriet had short, brown frizzy hair and sky-blue eyes that glistened in the faded streetlamp light. Sky, on the other hand, had a pure white fluffy coat (which got soaked in the cloud burst) and was the same pigment as a blanket of snow.

Harriet came across a mysterious house after her search for shelter, and there was a... Creaek! The ancient brown, wooden door swung open by the mighty force of the gust of wind. After a short pause of silence, a cloud of bats fluttered out of the door. Once the bats cleared off into the open, Harriet and Sky approached the entrance, and as they did so, they listened to the deserted house wail in agony. Harriet kept high alert, with her eyes wide open; Harriet's dog's bark was extremely loud, therefore it echoed back nearly instantly!

She was a statue as her eyes scanned the room when suddenly her pupils adjusted to the darkness, and she saw something... Someone was lurking in the shadows. Whoever it was, wore a cloak as dark as the midnight sky. Night was falling now, and she would be in hot water if she didn't leave for home. Her mum would be extremely worried.

"Who are you?" asked Harriet, quivering and uncertainly. She got no response, however, she heard: wolves howling, birds tweeting and death calling.

Then a voice in the dark replied, "Blood for wine, and flesh for bread; for dessert the dog's head." Harriet's heart was pounding, Sky was shivering. She ran, ran her fastest her feet could carry her, to the exit. Three... She was nearly there. Two... Was she going to make it? One... She made it! Bang! The door slammed shut! She was horror-struck but relieved.

Wonderful, Wary Wings

Today was a scorching summer's day. I was out and about in my garden, where I watched the trees sway calmly in a gentle breeze; the flowers joyfully dancing; busy bumble bees buzzing and a cluster of leaves zooming around like race cars. Best of all were the freshly plucked strawberries which delighted my taste buds; the sweet scent of the spectacular strawberries which was marvellously miraculous as it lingered in the air. Finally, the day had come to make my dreams come true: to fly like a bird...

I had invented wings. Not ordinary wings, wings for humans! It had long, arched, multi-coloured feathers protruding from the surface. The size was truly unbelievable, reaching out to approximately 1.5 metres in length. The time has arrived to test this magnificent beast! Immediately, I placed the massive wings on my back (it was extremely light despite its size). I was exhilarated. Three... (I was super nervous!) Two... (Was it going to work?) ONE! Now, there is no turning back, I was off!

I was a bird soaring through the air! It was amazing! It was wonderful! It was spectacular! The views utterly majestic, the beautiful scenery stretched out for miles! After gazing at the world below, I became exhausted for one reason: having to flap my wings incessantly. I was back, back in my garden which was alive, with energy flowing through the shrubbery which was shaking its hips whilst the flowers danced.

Creepy, cunning creature

The scintillating sun was soaring through the azure-blue sky, while Sophia was at a camp for a geography trip. Sophia's soft, smooth and silky blonde hair cascaded down her back like a waterfall. Her ocean-blue eyes glistened like stars in the midnight sky. Her clothes hung on her thin, skeletal frame since she was practically skin and bones. It was obvious that Sophia was a twig and had a growth spurt when she was young.

As soon as everyone popped out of their camps, Mrs Smith announced, "Our first task today is to go out and explore the wonders of the Earth (our home). Beware of the dangers, and don't go too far from camp. We'll meet back here after around 15 minutes or so." Thrilled at the thought of exploring, Sophia excitedly scrambled around in the woods when suddenly she spotted it.

It was an absurd looking creature with long, droopy arms. It ran... Sophia ran after it... She could hear a chorus of creatures, the wind whistling, a cluster of crispy, sycamore leaves crunch beneath her feet and the trees dancing. Out of the blue, it vanished. Sophia collapsed. Her ankle was in pain! "Where did it go? What was it?" pondered Sophie who was in a state of confusion.

Immediately, Sophia got up and hopped back to camp, despite the pain caused by her ankle. BANG! "What on Earth happened to you?" exclaimed Hannah, Sophia's friend, who dropped her mug, as well as her mouth.

"Umm... Long story short, I found an alien-like creature, and I fell down," claimed Sophia.

"Hahaha! Have you lost your mind? I believe the fell down part, because of the way you are walking and the leaves in your hair, but aliens? Can you be a little bit more serious?" laughed Hannah.

At last, she was back in her tent and put a plaster on her ankle. It was there...in the bushes. The alien! Sophia wisely refused to chase after it and remained inside the protection of her tent. Soon afterwards, she drifted off to sleep, regaining energy for the days ahead...

Writing Examples

The WORST day!

Amber woke up blissfully unaware that she was going to have the most treacherous day of her life so far. She had short black curly hair that looked like a bird's nest laid on a pillow since she hadn't washed her hair in a week. As she rose from her slumber, her eyelids finally revealed her honey brown eyes, which glimmered in the early morning or autumnal sunlight.

Reluctantly, she dragged herself out of her large, comfortable, double bed. Approaching the flight of wooden steps, she slipped on a rouge shoe and tumbled down the spiky steps; this was the start to the terrible day Amber was going to experience. As she screamed in agony, her caring mother rushed to her darling daughter's side. While sprinting (to see what the commotion was), her mother's coffee cup escaped her grasp and landed on Amber's slender torso. Poor Amber was deeply depressed.

On her way to school, she remembered she had forgotten to do her homework. What was she going to do? Remembering all those horrid punishments she had received, her stomach ached. Oblivious of her surroundings, she slipped. SPLASH! Like a pig in the mud, she sat there, disheartened. What was she going to do? What was there to do?

"My WORD!" exclaimed her teacher, "You didn't have a bath in mud, did you? Well, anyways, where's your homework?"

Terror struck Amber's face... She was about to receive the worst punishment in her life... Her heart sank as she trudged her way to her desk.

Daisy Smith

She's a 17 with jet-black hair and emerald-green eyes; she was with her family, camping in the woods during the summer.

It all started when she went on a search to find the perfect spot to write in her journal. As she roamed around the woods, sinister grey clouds began to invade the skies. Suddenly, she came across a creepy, cold cave. Her spine tingled and the hairs on her neck instantly stood up. Despite that, she went in…

Inside the cave, she sat peacefully and wrote. The silence was deafening, but it didn't last any longer. As something or someone disturbed it, the sound of footsteps echoed through the cave. It stopped. She assumed she had imagined it all.

Out of the blue, she felt something on her back. She was certain! Then the footsteps came again. Louder. At this point, she was horrified and too stunned to speak. She got up and ran. Ran and ran. She was back where she started as her journal was still there, sleeping on the floor. She was horror-struck. She couldn't believe her eyes. Tears trickled down her face as she fell to the floor disheartened. She was trapped.

We only know what happened because of her journal. Which was found after a week of endlessly searching for her. Only the journal is left of her as she was never seen again…

The Day I Met the Queen

The day I met Queen Elizabeth II, who reigned over England, was a spectacular day.

After quarrelling with my sister, I heard a loud knock at the door. It was the taxi driver. Next destination, Buckingham Palace! As I looked out of the window, I could see blocks of flats which reached up to the sky, walls sprayed with graffiti and streets bustling with tourists who eagerly waited at the golden gates of Buckingham Palace.

The sky was clear blue, with not a single cloud in sight and the sizzling sun sailing across. I was surprised by the enormous building that stood in front of me: its shadow cast down on me intimidatingly. There seemed to be millions and millions of windows! As the glossy, green grass swayed in the wind merrily, the large wooden door swung open.

Hastily, I joined the never-ending queue. I could see the other guests being greeted by the two tall servants. I was handed a badge which was encrusted with the finest diamonds I had ever seen. Portraits of previous monarchs hung on the walls. It looked like they were smiling gleefully at me. Patiently, I waited for my turn to enter the grand throne room, where the Queen was residing that day. It was dawning on me that I was inches away from meeting one of the most well-known figures in the world. I felt anxious, terrified and terror-stricken at the thought of meeting Queen Elizabeth II.

There she was! The Queen! She was wearing a resplendent, ruby-red robe, which was utterly stunning! The Queen! Her crown peacefully sat on her shiny silver hair, which was extremely curly!

I was over the moon when she exclaimed, "Hello! Please, please take a seat, what's your name?" I was speechless – was the Queen really talking to me?

"I-I am N-Naima, pleasure to meet you, your Majesty!" I replied, trying my best to be as formal as possible.

"My personal assistant informed me of your visit. I have also heard that you won a lottery. How did you feel when you found out? Oh, and please do have a sip of tea," stated the Queen. Then, we had a private conversation which was informative.

The day I met the petite and powerful queen was a surreal experience. It was the most marvellous day of my life, and this magnificent memory will never leave my mind.

Crystal Cove Cave!

It was a splendid summer's day, as the scintillating sun soared in the azure-blue sky. I was at the beach with all my school friends (including their dogs). We were all there for one reason only: a crystal hunt. It was instructed by an oddly fashioned guy – who had a long grey beard which looked like a bird's nest. The peculiar man wore an electric blue cloak, dark as the night, and a matching crooked hat.

"Before we start, here is a clue. It lies within a chest and don't touch the rest! Okay, now we're ready. You may begin!" he bellowed. We were all baffled by his bizarre speech but didn't question it.

Eagerly, I began rummaging around as Emi (my dog, who was a pom-pom) sniffed around going all over the place. All I could hear was the sounds of the waves hitting the shingles on the shore. I gazed around as the water moved from side to side... peacefully. The silence broke when I heard Emi call; it was only then that I realised everyone had vanished, but it didn't matter to me. A cave! Emi had found a cave! As I took one step inside, I became a statue! There were tapering stalactites as sharp as a knife glued on the ceiling.

However, things got even better. Marvellous magical crystals rose from the ground, and soon after, there were crystals in all shapes and sizes scattered all over the place. "Wow," I cried. "Woof woof," Emi replied. I was flabbergasted, dumbfounded and amazed. The incessant sound of drip... drip... could be heard from a mile away. Suddenly, I spotted it! The eerie golden glow caught my eye and courageously, Emi went in to fetch it. I was inches away from laying my hands on the shiny objects when suddenly I remembered what the mysterious man had said, and it all came together in my head and began to make sense.

I had won!

A day in my life as the Queen!

I would love to be the queen because then you are: well respected, have responsibility, are capable of making your own decisions and a great piece of history. Despite everything I own this is one thing in my long, lengthy list that I have not yet acquired.

My first day as the queen:

The vague sound of birds singing lingered up my ears as I leapt in the air like a bullet due to the sudden wakening by my maid. Sophia (as she was known) served me my delectable, mouth-watering and irresistible breakfast. Almost exactly after breakfast, I was dressed by Emma – another maid – which was unusual as I normally got changed on my own, so this was a change from my normal routine. When I peered in the mirror, I was a statue. I was flabbergasted! I was wearing a resplendent red robe, which was magnificent and appealing.

In the latter half of the day, I took my cute pom-pom like dog on a stroll in the green, grassy gardens, when suddenly my butler signalled me to come. Immediately I gracefully approached him. "There is a royal ball, and you are required to attend it. I informed you yesterday my majesty," claimed my butler.

"Sorry I forgot! I am on my way," I replied.

I was escorted by my bodyguards to the ball where they mysteriously vanished like a cloud that went poof! It was amazing! I LOVED it! It was the time of my life! There was dancing, music, laughter. It was pure enjoyment. Best of all I was surrounded by friends, family and fun. Even though they weren't my real friends and family, they were still nicer than my real ones. It was all epic... Was the day really going to be over?

I was exhausted; my eyes fell shut and I drifted off to sleep knowing I would wake up to being the inquisitive, little girl I was...

Different Dimension

Samidi was an inquisitive girl for her age and very determined. However, she looked very peculiar! Her static brown hair had a mind of its own and made her look as if she had been electrocuted. Even if she brushed it down it would shoot up like lightning. She was literally a twig with eyes as blue as the ocean.

Despite having parents that loved her more than the world itself, she was sent to the countryside – to live with her Aunt Kendal due to the current outbreak of smallpox (mainly in the urban areas). There was an unusual feeling that tingled up your spine when you took one step into the house. As if ghostly spirits were haunting the place.

"This is your room," exclaimed Aunt Kendal. "Oh, and don't try opening the tiny door in the corner," warned Aunt Kendal sternly.

Obviously, Samidi had to take a tiny peek! She searched everywhere but unfortunately couldn't find the key when suddenly she encountered a mini box covered by an intricate design that tempted her to open it. What an unusual place to hide a key? Samidi thought to herself.

But why did her aunt try to conceal it? wondered Samidi thoughtfully. "Well, I guess I'll just have to find out myself."

She missed her parents dearly, and the racket the cars made by the roads. It was like she had been teleported into another dimension! It was so strange without her family that always used to be by her side, no matter what situation they were in.

BAM! The door opened with such ferocity that the windy winds whooshed past her hair like a thunder bolt. As excitement took control she leapt into the tunnel like a frog. Where was she?

It was dull. It was bleak. The question was, where was she and how was she going to get out? She was only ten and didn't know what to do next.

There was an approaching shadow that charged forwards. What was she going to do next?
There was an abrupt pause...

Kisali Wijesekara

Description

My tips:

- When writing a description, use POSAM to remember to use personification, onomatopoeia, similes, alliteration and metaphors.

- A description is a very important part of story writing. You can describe a character or a setting.

- Use appropriate punctuation such as exclamation marks and brackets not speech marks.

- Try using expanded noun phrases and the power of three when writing a description.

My imaginary friend

Her eyes are as blue as the crystal-clear ocean that crashes on the craggy coastline; sometimes, if you're lucky, you can catch a glimpse of it! They are like diamonds, glistening in the sunshine. Her name is Liz, and she has stunning blondish-brown, bouncy hair that cascades down her back endlessly. Liz is lanky and slim with long droopy arms that hung from her joints in between her sides and shoulders.

It often looked like she was a skeleton frame with clothes hanging from it. Her smooth, soft skin was as pale as a ghost's, and it was unbelievably flawless. Whenever she smiles, you can't take your eyes off her (Liz's teeth stand out because of their distinctive white pigment), it would always light up the whole world!

She is also inquisitive and quite the investigator. If someone commits a crime, she'll be the first to arrive at the crime scene. You can always rely on her to figure out who the culprit is. Under her cloak of beauty, she conceals her intelligence and bravery.

Liz is an outstanding singer, with a voice like an angel's, and an utterly appealing melody that flows within her songs. Her songs are like beautiful bird songs with low and high pitch voices included. She is destined to become a super singing star and I guarantee she will have a successful career, with a bright future.

Camping in the woods

One hazy morning, the birds sang their long, lovely melodies as they sat on the tall, towering trees – which were covered in a mountain of snow from top to bottom. I sat solemnly by the fire as it roared and crackled incessantly. Tapering stalactites – which were razor sharp – hung above me like shark teeth glued to the ceiling.

The ice walls closed in on me; they were mirrors that reflected my complexion in them. I held my marshmallow above the fire (which hissed like a snake) as I rubbed my hands with the wooden, brown stick in between them. The cave was small. The cave was cramped. The cave was ice-cold. Despite the lovely aroma of my marshmallow, there was still a putrid, rancid and horrid odour that lingered in the cave.

As I stared at the woods, I was almost definite that I heard a crunch. Something or someone had set foot on the blanket of snow that camouflaged the ancient pine trees. This concealed any evidence of a tundra existing beyond it. Honestly, it was stunning, utterly stunning! I couldn't believe my eyes! It was… amazing!

Suddenly, wolves began howling and growling… What was lurking in the shadows of this snow-white forest?

The Ancient Forest!

Deep in the shadows of this ancient and mythical forest, lies a chorus of creatures that roam around peacefully. In time, all that can be heard is the roar of the gusty, perishing breeze that haunts this magical forest. A flock of birds fly into the horizon and vanish suddenly. As the sun sets, the sky fills with a variety of colours: rose – pink, sea – blue, orange ...

Anyone that harms the life of this spectacular forest will be shown no mercy or forgiveness. As the sun rises from its deep sleep, filling the air with specks of gold dust, below the tall, towering trees that overshadow each other, the wind gently picks up the luscious, long leaves pretending they're a race car that zooms them up and down through the dense air. While the wind was screaming at the leaves, the delicate flowers danced till their petals dropped off. Through the trees that whispered to each other, an eerie neon yellow glow lights up the whole woodlands. Tenacious blossoms of bluebells glistened by the bright sunlight; the aroma spread everywhere.

The bustling, busy streets of London!

One scorching day, a horde of people trudged around searching for household, miscellaneous items, and succulent food. There were deafening booms of the sea of people who waited in never-ending queues. The unnoticeable diseased rats scatted around the narrow road and were trampled by the cynical humans. In the clear blue sky, the birds swooped and soared over the citizens of London. The tramps were pleaded to move or else they would be beaten to their fate! As for the rich, they would help themselves to whatever treasures they could get their moisturised hands on! The treacherous aroma of the distinct smell of smoke from nearby industries spread through the air.

My Mayan character

His name was, Theo, he had jet-black hair, which was concealed by a multi-coloured feathery hat. Unlike the other warriors, he was very tall (7 feet approximately) therefore his head stuck out in any crowd, as he towered above everyone effortlessly. His muscular arms were covered in tattoos that danced around his entire body. He stood fiercely wielding his spear, as the light breeze rustled his feathers like leaves.

Theo was an honest, kind warrior who cared for others, especially his loved ones. He was a man of justice. If you harmed him or his family, be warned you have something terrible coming your way.

The Ice Queen

Behind the snow-white walls of Winter Palace, a disastrous, catastrophic Ice Queen sat back-straight on the utterly magnificent, stunning, and majestic throne (which was covered by an intricate design). She has smooth, soft and silky hair, which cascaded down her back like a golden waterfall. Her eyes are stars stolen from the midnight sky; her dress is showered with hand-stitched diamonds as it hangs over her thin skeleton frame. When ominous grey clouds invaded the sky, a smirk can certainly be spotted on her pale face, which looks like a phantom.

She is cruel... wicked... horrid... the worst person you can ever imagine. If you ever dared to look her dead in the eyes, you will instantly turn into a statue. Picturing her in your mind tearing your heart into two. If this wicked woman was ever to walk past you, she is guaranteed to be accompanied by her guards, who follow her in a triangular formation and she would certainly be side by side with her magnificent silver staff, which always chases after her.

Kisali Wijesekara

News Report

My tips:

- When writing a news report, use A FOREST to remember to use alliteration, facts, opinion, rhetorical questions/ repetition, emotive language, statistics and triplets.

- Remember the 5w's: who, what, where, when and why. An extra one to remember is how.

- Use as much advanced vocabulary as possible.

- Use at least two eye-witness quotes.

- Remember to use formal language.

- You can always start with 'Last week, any date, this incident that occurred...'

Peril in Paris. Enormous Earthquake!

Yesterday, Monday 12th May 2021, an earthquake struck Paris (the capital of France). Scientists and the government officials were all horrified by this terrible, tragic event. Government parties requested that all citizens should evacuate their homes immediately.

Predominantly, search parties have reported that no bodies have been discovered yet beneath the fallen city, which once had tall, towering and colossal skyscrapers that reached into the azure-blue sky. Although now they are a stack of crumbly rocks. Government research proves that 95% of the people in Paris evacuated; this means 5% may still be buried under the mountain of stone.

Ruby Smith, 35, a witness of the earthquake, cried, "M-my house fell to the ground in the blink of an eye! As fast as the wind! I'm utterly devastated. I-I have nowhere to go and seek shelter anymore! What can I do? All my prized possessions were inside of my marvellous home!"

Mike King, 47, who evacuated the heart-breaking event, claimed that he was lucky to have fled his home with his family just in time, as he made it out of the city with only a minor fracture in his ankle whilst trying to escape the clutches of the unfortunate earthquake.

In conclusion, the effects of this earthquake are yet to be fully discovered. The government is working on a new plan to build and take the architecture of the city to new heights. This new architecture that has been proposed is aiming to withstand further earthquakes and escape destruction of the city.

Terrible Tragedy on a School Trip

Last week, it was reported that a whole class of children (in year five) did not manage to return from the Jurassic era. Travelling to the Jurassic era may sound absurd, but with the help of Super Time Travel – STT – the class succeeded in time travelling to what is now known as the dinosaur period. Many people think the children are dead; this may be true as most of the dinosaurs are carnivores.

After three days of effortlessly searching for clues on the disappearance of the class, it was confirmed that there had been a malfunction within the teleporting machine. It was unfortunate that the children were unable to find the portal again to return. However, it is possible that the class travelled back in time to when The Big Bang occurred. If so, this would have caused them to wipe-out with the massive and minuscule beasts. How dreadful!

Mrs Smith, 48, the current head teacher at Medway Primary school claimed, "I am not responsible for the loss of these children as all parents were required to sign the contract, which clearly states what might possibly go wrong!"

Parents on the other hand, accused STT of sending their beloved children to their doom. Melody, 28, mum of two claims that she burst into streams of tears as soon as she found out the heart-breaking news and completely blamed Super Time Travel for not being super. Many other parents are consumed by worry and grief and spend all day grieving due to the awful tragedy that has befallen their children.

It is rumoured that a court date has been set and all future STT travel is banned until there is an outcome. The families of the students missing are taking a class action suit. This is a story that is sure to have many more twists and turns.

Dixie's dinosaur discovery!

Yesterday, it was confirmed that eleven-year-old Dixie discovered a new historic creature believed to have come from the dinosaur period from 65 million years ago. The skeleton was dug up by Dixie, who was also accompanied by her friend, Emily. Dixie had revealed a prehistoric dinosaur lair that may have been home to many dinosaurs from this new species. The creature had once lived in what is now known as Duke, situated in the West region of Kent.

Nature has preserved it in the most delicate way, revealing the exact body structure without any flaws or cracks. The creature is named after Dixie as she was the one to discover it. Its official name is Dixiesaurous. Dixie's findings will improve dinosaur theories and help reveal the truth of their past lives before extinction. It may also be the key in figuring out the true reason for their disappearance.

Dixie Dame, 11, stated that she was exploring the caves with her friend, and she spotted a bone which was as sharp as a knife protruding from the soft, smooth soil and curiosity took over her. She began to dig and dig. There it was, the Dixiesaurous – the dinosaur she had discovered.

The local museum has bought the ancient fossil for one hundred thousand pounds from Dixie, and it is proudly featured in the museum. Professor Jay claimed, "I believe the skeleton is approximately 65 million years old and is in the best condition as it was well preserved."

The entire area surrounding the cave is currently unavailable to the public due to excavations being made as it is now an archaeological site.

ಶಿಂಚಿಶಿ

Kisali Wijesekara

Report

My tips:

- When writing a report, use A FOREST to remember to use alliteration, facts, opinions, rhetorical questions / repetition, emotive language, statistics and triplets.

- Use a variety of punctuations.

- Don't use eyewitnesses as you won't need them.

- Try get the reader's attention by making it interesting and by using loads of adjectives.

- You can still start with 'Last week, any date, this incident that occurred…'

Kisali Wijesekara

Two Peculiar Planets!

Last week, Monday 27th May 2021, two astronauts came back from space with massive news. Two planets have been discovered outside of our entire galaxy; they are in fact very unlike our planets and differ in many ways. The official names have already been declared: Diamond and Dusk.

Diamond:

Diamond is an out-of-this-world planet which is extremely cold with freezing temperatures that fluctuate between minus five to approximately minus thirty degrees. Chilly or what? One astronaut (Jim Smith) claims that it was like setting foot on an iceberg. It is twice the size of Jupiter.

On planet Diamond, the clouds are frozen – on the outside that is – but they are inflated with helium, meaning they are floating. Plus, this is evidence that life may have existed on this planet as the temperature must have had a significant increase for the ice to have vaporised. This may be the reason why the planet is blue when viewed from above.

Dusk:

This marvellous, miraculous and magical planet is named after its ring of dust. Planet Dusk is an orange planet as it's a very dry and barren planet. It's in fact the shape of a star, which is very peculiar for a planet. It has a gravitational field and large crates on the surface of the planet which is proof that life existed on Planet Dusk. The crates are where rivers used to flow but only small pools of water remain today. Scientists estimate that Planet Dusk is approximately twice the size of Earth.

The government recently announced that two rocket ships will be sent to both Dusk and Diamond in the following year to conduct some tests to try learning what species may have previously inhabited the planets and if humans can live there in the future.

Kisali Wijesekara

Diaries

My tips:

- When writing a diary, use POSAM to remember to use personification, onomatopoeia, similes, alliteration and metaphors.

- Use advanced vocabulary that fit in the context as usual.

- Write the date on the top right corner.

- Remember to use informal language.

- Do not forget it must be in first person.

- Don't use speech marks in a diary.

Kisali Wijesekara

7/8/2020

Dear Diary,

I can't believe the time has come – tomorrow we're finally moving house! I can't wait! Although I'll quite miss this house dearly; at least I won't have to move school. If I did, then my life would be over! Seriously! I wonder how the new house will look. Is it gargantuan? Or is it miniature? I have been packing: my clothes, hat, shoes, toys, and miscellaneous items that have sentimental value etc. Ekkk... Honestly, I'm bursting to see my new house already!

8/8/2020

Dear Diary,

Today was the big move – the new house is colossal, bigger than I could ever imagine for a house. A gust of excitement struck my face when I first laid eyes on the gigantic building. Although, as I took one step into the house, my joy faded away. It was bleak, boring and dull (my room especially). There were: creaky floorboards, crusty painted walls, and a deafening silence. The dilapidated house gave me ghostly chills.

Writing Examples

9/8/2020

Dear Diary,

I finally settled down (confining myself in my bedroom). What was rather peculiar was the key I found on the floor. Why on Earth would someone leave keys on the floor – which creaked in agony? I was a statue when I spotted it. However, after hours of searching for the door it unlocks, I couldn't find it! How bizarre! I'm utterly baffled!

10/8/2020

Dear Diary,

I found the door – at the back of my bedroom. I opened it. It was empty. Pitch-black. I courageously strode in. BANG! The door slammed shut! My heart was pounding as fast as lightning. I screamed as loud as a lion's roar. It was spine-tingling. Boom...Out of the blue, there was my lovely mother who came to the rescue! Thank goodness she saved me. After recovering from the shock, I seem to have lost my opinion of the house; I don't know what to think anymore... my life lesson learnt: never wander around on your own.

Kisali Wijesekara

20/5/2020

Dear Diary,

Guess what? You won't believe it! On my way to school, I fell inside a hole within an oak tree and found my way to another world! I know, I know I must sound insane, but I guarantee I'm not hallucinating! They call it 'The Upside Down'! (I'll come to detail further on.)

It was an ordinary day of school – as usual – apart from the A* I got in my writing, sorry if I sound too pompous. Anyways, that all changed on my way back home… I was cautiously strolling on the pebbly path, watching the trees murmur to each other whilst the flowers were dancing in a melodic rhythm, when suddenly I spotted a robin. What's the big deal about spotting a robin you might ask? The fact that it flew into a hollow tree trunk and never flew back out! Obviously, I was baffled and went to investigate what was going on…

Sprinting over, I peered inside, I lost balance and fell right in! My eyes were locked shut preparing for the wooden surface to smash into my fat face. After a couple of seconds, I opened my eyes and gazed around. I thought I had died and that I was in heaven, but there it was… The robin! "How on Earth did I get here?" I pondered. "Welcome to The Upside Down!" stated the Robin. My eyes widened; my jaw dropped wide open! It was talking! WICKED, right?

I could see: a flock of birds soaring in the coral pink sky; a blanket of leaves sitting on the soft soil; red blossoms floating in the air; and a chorus of creatures lurking in the woods. It was-out-of-this-world! It was majestic and stunning. I am definitely visiting again!

☙☙☙

Kisali Wijesekara

Letters

My tips:

- When writing a letter, remember to use A FOREST: alliteration, facts, opinion, rhetorical questions/repetition, exaggeration, statistics and triplets/power of three.
- Use year 5 & 6 vocabulary such as guarantee, occur, immediately or individual.
- Write the date on the top right corner.
- Do not forget it must be in first person.
- You address must be written in the top right corner.
- If you know the name of the person, you're writing to, you end with 'yours sincerely' but if you don't know who it is then you end with 'yours faithfully'.

Kisali Wijesekara

3 Park Lane,
Rochester,
ME1 2 BQJ.

3/02/2021

Mrs Murphy,
New Horizon Children's Academy,
Chatham.
ME4 5ND.

Dear Mrs Murphy,

I'm writing to you because I have heard you are considering allowing the year five children to go to Chessington World of Adventures. There are many reasons as to why this trip will be beneficial.

Despite the many changes, the children have worked exceptionally hard. The children have faced many challenges such as lockdown, online learning, and a change of routine. During lockdown, children have not communicated and socialised as much as they normally would. Going to Chessington World Adventures will help to develop these skills. Therefore, I believe that the trip to Chessington World of Adventure will enhance their social skills. Wouldn't you want that for the children of your school?

Another reason why this could be important is because it could be considered educational. Each individual child will be provided with their own personal maps. This links into Geography, (which is important because it links to life skills), as the children will be reading a map to get from ride to ride. Plus, during the trip, children will have to calculate how much they spend – forcing themselves to do some maths. Don't you think this would be an educational trip?

As you may know, the children have been lacking exercise since they had to confine themselves inside their house and did not go out as much as they normally would. A visit to Chessington World of Adventures would be an excellent way to get the children out and about in broad daylight. If children do not exercise, they could become obese, unhealthy and they would be more likely to have a shorter life expectancy. Would a tiny trip to Chessington hurt?

Some may say that this trip could be potentially dangerous for children our age. However, I have already considered this problem and come up with a variety of solutions. One way to solve this issue is ensuring that children are in small groups and are frequently counted. Each group will be assisted by multiple adults, meaning that fewer accidents will occur. With these measures taken, children will be less likely to be put in danger.

In conclusion, I hope you take my request seriously and take this into consideration. Thank you for having a look at this. I look forward to your reply.

Yours sincerely,
Kisali.

Kisali Wijesekara

4 Bark Lane,
Gillingham,
ME1 2 BQJ.

12/11/20

Dear Melody ,

How are you? Have you enjoyed your weekend? I was wondering whether you would be interested in joining Dance Club with me. It would be a great opportunity for you to learn some new names, socialise and make more friends. We both can also learn to dance as gracefully as a swan.

Plus, it will be amazing! We'll have a blast! It'll be the best experience of our life. I was informed that there is an upcoming competition. We could compete after a little bit of practice. Wouldn't that be incredible?

Through listening to rumours I found out there would be parties just for dancers in our school. I guarantee there will be cake, because if there's a party, there's going to be cake and I know you like cake. Did I mention there would be medals awarded to dancers? It will be held in front of the whole school! EKKK! Exciting, right?

Guess what? We even get to skip math class – which we both agreed was boring – for extra practice. Oh yeah, and I forgot to mention that the costume is not only free, but they also look like an opulent dress fit for a princess.

Moreover, they are encrusted with hand stitched diamonds and glossy green emeralds.

I hope you consider coming and I know you won't let me down as I won't join without you. I'm looking forward to seeing your response,

Your best friend,
Kisali.

P.S. Dance classes on Monday – after school – and Tuesday to Friday during math class.

Kisali Wijesekara

> 41 Cross Road,
> Sevenoaks,
> Kent,
> ME4 6NZ.
>
> Monday 25th May 2021

Gary Will,
Secretary of State for Education.
Kent Council
Kent.
MR6 7DE.

Dear Mr Will,

I am writing to politely request a reduction of school days; instead of five days of school, I was thinking perhaps four days. My reasons are listed below:

Predominantly, increasing time on the weekend will allow children to rest, relax and refresh as you may know this is crucial for children to have effective learning. It has been scientifically proven that 95% of children who have longer holidays or weekends have better memory – which I am certain you are aware of. Do you not want us to be better learners?

Furthermore, extending the weekend will enable children to spend more quality time with their families and bond with siblings, otherwise their bridges will burn. A three-day weekend is also long enough to go on a holiday for a day or two with time to unpack and regain energy for the next day.

Consequently, children will have better memory and they will be ready for learning, therefore smarter.

Take Sweden as an example. They don't start school until seven. However, they have produced some of the world's smartest people. Like this, England will create better learners. By better learners I mean smarter children, which means better education. As the Education Secretary, this is a great way of stepping up and showing the world your great ideas. Do you not want that?

In conclusion, I would really appreciate if you could grant my wish or at least take this into consideration. Thank you very much for taking time to read this.

Yours sincerely,
Kisali
(A year five pupil.)

32 Windy Road,
Chatham,
Kent,
ME4 6NZ.

Thursday 11th March 2021

10 Big Boss Lane,
Gillingham,
Kent,
ME8 6NX.

Dear Boris Johnson,

I'm writing to you in order to improve the use of internet in the hands of children below the age of eleven. Maybe even a new law be put in place addressing this issue.

Predominantly there are a variety of reasons as to why children use the internet. However, not everything is age appropriate, and recent research scientifically proves that 85% of children come across inappropriate things whether it is: adverts, social medias, profile pages, etc. This is appalling and unacceptable – precautions must be taken seriously.

On the one hand, many children tend to make online friends, but the person on the other side of the screen might not be who they say they are. This is also a possibility of being stalked, which can be extremely dangerous and lead to identities being revealed or worse.

To enhance my previous point, there have been an astounding number of cases of when children have been watching 15 + movies. To reduce the number of cases children should have apps that restrict inappropriate films (like YouTube Kids).

Lastly, parents have had many unfortunate accidents where their children have accidentally purchased a range of miscellaneous items that cost hundreds, perhaps even thousands of pounds on Amazon, eBay, etc.

In conclusion, I strongly believe action is essential to be taken immediately and that a law should be considered on behalf of this matter. I'm looking forward to seeing the changes that you make. Thank you for taking your time to read this.

Yours sincerely,
Kisali.

Kisali Wijesekara

20 Fantastic Road,
Chatham,
Kent,
ME4 6NZ.

Sunday 2nd May 2021

Mrs. Smith, Head teacher,
Marvellous Academy,
Park Crescent,
Chatham,
ME9 7NY.

Dear Mrs. Smith,

I am writing on behalf of the Year 5 school trip that took place on the 30th of April 2021. I am aware of some unfortunate incidents that have occurred. My daughter was shivering with horror when she returned home. She told me what dreadful things had happened to her and some other children, during the trip.

First, she was locked in a bathroom (located in the Southeast of the Hampton Court Hotel). I was also informed that she missed the tour of the palace which was the main experience as well as the royal garden views. Imogen- my beloved daughter – was stuck for approximately four hours! How horrendous! This transpired due to the lax guide and the teacher, Mr Max and Mrs Carter. Imogen claims they had been too busy with their conversation and they forgot a headcount! I am appalled by this utterly ridiculous behaviour!!

Furthermore, when Imogen's peers returned to the hotel room and helped her out and carried on with their trip, at the village, they were accompanied by a mad hatter, who I assumed to be drunk as he started throwing rocks at them incessantly. This is incontrovertible as Imogen and her classmates have lumps and bruises. Again, the teachers didn't even attempt protecting/defending the children. The class used strenuous efforts to escape the clutches of the old man.

In conclusion, I expect a partial refund as my child missed the main parts of the trip and was severely injured. Thank you for taking time to read my letter. I look forward to your prompt reply.

Yours sincerely,
Rachel (Imogen's mum)

Kisali Wijesekara

Leaflets

My tips:

- When writing an information leaflet, remember to use A FOREST.

- Use subheadings to separate information.

- Do not forget, it must be informative.

- End with a conclusion to sum up everything.

- Use alliteration or rhyme for the title (optional).

- Use a variety of punctuation…

- Don't forget to use wow words.

Annoying Adults!

To all the parents across the world, this leaflet is to guide you to stop being annoying, embarrassing and distracting. We love and appreciate you for everything you have done. Sometimes, you can be a little absurd but not to worry, that may be fixed! Read on and you shall learn about all the solutions...

Behaviour when guests or friends come

It is extremely frustrating when you act as if we are tiny, little babies. For example, when my mum picked up my (seven-year-old) friend who was crying and rocked her in her arms. It was indeed very sweet as she started laugh-crying, but I was teased for roughly a month! Appalling or what! Instead tell her not to cry sweetly and try make a joke that's not funny so that she'll laugh at how bad the joke was.

How to dress

After school, don't come dressed as a polar bear when the super, scorching sun is floating in the beautiful baby-blue sky! Wear something appropriate according to the weather. Isn't that what you normally tell us?

How to act with people having a conversation with you

To begin with, stop with the gestures as they look abnormal! Act according to your age and please stop with the laughing, especially the fake laughs because they sound horrendous! If you don't, you'll burn the bridges between you and your children. However, don't worry you can easily fix that with a couple of reminders.

We cannot explain how grateful we are even if you are really embarrassing. If you follow my tips, I can guarantee you will be less annoying. Sometimes, it's best to be a statue when people come so you don't need to worry.

Healthy lifestyle for Children and Students!

Do you want to be healthy, fit, and strong? Here's a guide on how to stay/ become healthy:

Exercise

Exercising plays a vital role in helping you stay in shape (being healthy). It is essential to exercise every day! 95% of doctors advise to aim to be out and about for 40 minutes, minimum. This will ensure you keeping fit and active. It will also keep your blood moving, with your heart pumping. Exercising will also help you have a longer life expectancy. Don't you want to live longer?

Eating habits

As an ordinary child/ student, it is normal to be continuously munching on delectable, succulent snacks. However, it is crucial to limit the amount of junk food you consume. Otherwise, a great amount of junk food can lead to obesity, which can be extremely unhealthy as you become vulnerable to diabetes (type 2). You should try stick to a balanced diet and make sure you eat your fruit and veg.

Negatives

If you don't act now, you could: become obese, have a short life expectancy, have decayed teeth and suffer from diabetes, etc. This is part of a long list of frightening, terrifying and miserable things that may occur. We highly recommend beginning a healthy lifestyle in order to keep yourself healthy and strong.

In conclusion, I strongly believe you should have a healthy lifestyle. From my perspective, unhealthy habits aren't worth their consequences.

Be fit, don't quit!

Are you gaining a substantial amount of weight? Well, guess what...? We have the perfect solution! Be fit don't quit (BFDQ) is what you need! We encourage and support you to work out at our gym; this will start your heart pumping and your blood racing.

This opportunity will enable you to take classes with others as well as your highly trained supervisor. You will be given breaks – around 8 to 10 minutes – which will allow you to socialise and make friends with others. Don't delay, come today and if you miss it, you miss out!

Exercising is essential to enhance your immune system and extend your life expectancy. It will also prevent obesity, heart diseases and diabetes. Therefore, you are recommended to join a gym before something unpleasant occurs.

Did you know BFDQ provide a range of equipment ranging over 100. There is also a stall where refreshments are available; don't panic if you forgot your bottle for a day or two.

Join BFDQ Now! You are guaranteed to have an unforgettable experience and you won't regret your decision!

Call: 7307 078441

Price: £10 (per class)

Writing Examples

Get your first lesson for FREE!

Bag a bargain at www.gymking.com

Kisali Wijesekara

Argument

My tips:

- When writing an argument, remember to use A FOREST.

- Make sure to check if it's one sided or two.

- End with a conclusion to sum up everything.

- If it's two sided, then state your opinion in the introduction and in the conclusion.

- Use fronted adverbials.
  example: Firstly, Predominantly, Finally

Should Uniform be Worn at School?

In this controversial argument, I shall be discussing both pros and cons of wearing school uniform. Personally, I think children should wear school uniform. What do you think? Before you decide on this commonly debated topic, first read through this balanced argument; then confirm your opinion...

Predominantly, children can get bullied. Schools that make uniform essential prevent discrimination from occurring. This has been proven by government research as 95% of schools that don't necessarily require school uniform have shown multiple signs of bullying – often due to the child's choice of clothing. Therefore, school uniform is the perfect solution to decrease the chance of being bullied! Do you want these innocent children to get bullied for what they wear?

On the other hand, uniforms can be uncomfortable. Children who have sensory issues may find certain materials of clothing uncomfortable, such as: blazers, tight ties, neck collars and skirts. Similarly, children with ADD (attention deficiency disorder) may also find this very distracting. It is not fair for these children to have to wear school uniform. They can become extremely traumatic, which can cause stress for parents/carers. This can be unhealthy to deal with every day. Would you want to be a stressed parent every morning?

However, you won't have to go shopping regularly. Children with school uniform will only need two to three sets of clothing which will last approximately a term.

If your school doesn't require wearing uniform, then you must buy clothes more often. This could be a problem for the parents who work most of the time and have little spare time left on their hands.

In conclusion, I think school uniform should be compulsory and beneficial except for students who are diagnosed with medical issues (severe sensory issues).

Is Teaching Online Better than Teaching in a Classroom?

In this argument, I shall be examining both pros and cons of this commonly debated topic I think teaching in classrooms is more effective and I will explain why further on. What do you think? Before confirming your opinion on this intriguing argument, first read through this balanced debate and then decide...

Predominantly, children all over the world can learn from the same teacher wherever you are. Additionally, even if you go on holiday as long as you have a device you can access your online learning. And if you are unavailable to attend a lesson it can be recorded and viewed multiple times. Is this not so very convenient?

On the other hand, online learning prevents any illnesses and viruses (such as covid-19) from spreading. In fact, it could even save people's lives! If children go to school, they will pass potentially dangerous illnesses to each other, and it may eventually pass to elderly grandparents who are vulnerable to these monstrous viruses and could perhaps even die from it! Do you want these innocent people to die due to our choices?

Online learning is more beneficial. After all, there are less disturbances – all of the children's mikes are under the teacher's control, and screens turned off, meaning children cannot pull faces whether they're humorous or disturbing.

Although the Internet may have some difficulties – sometimes this occurs because of the weather or poor connection. If the teacher's Internet is not working the whole class will not be able to learn. Wouldn't it be unfair for these eager learners?

I strongly believe teaching in classrooms is more beneficial. This is because children will develop other skills such as social interaction with peers and teachers (this may come in very useful in the future). Even though the lives of humans are incredibly important I still believe that children should go to school to learn.

බටඃ

Articles

My tips:

- When writing an article, remember to use A FOREST especially statistics to make it realistic.
- Use a catchy title as much as possible.
- Start using words with a hyphen such as 'life-threatening'.
- Use formal language.
- Remember to always use parentheses.

Pandemic!

It is very clear that COVID-19 has majorly impacted our lives. Disrupting our usual daily routines, we have gone through a great deal throughout the year.

During lockdown, many things dramatically changed as we had restrictions, schools shutting down, clubs decreasing and many more. 95% of children confined themselves to their rooms (this has been confirmed through government research). Means children could not communicate and socialise with their friends, which can lead them to isolation making them anti-social.

Due to government restrictions, people ranging from 10 to 50 years old were not getting as much exercise as they normally would. This is extremely unhealthy for the human body – making themselves vulnerable to viruses such as COVID-19. This may occur as all sports facilities and gyms are unavailable currently.

Coronavirus has affected us in many ways now that lockdown has eased. Many adults are advised to wear face protection to prevent spreading of this deadly virus. Unfortunately, the death toll continues to fluctuate above a thousand!

It's obvious that our lives have immensely changed over the months, and that it's far from the ordinary for us. Have you been affected by this wicked, life-threatening and heartless disease?

Fact file

My tips:

- When writing a fact file, remember to use A FOREST.

- Include what the subjects eat/drink, habitats and their appearance.

- Use colons and semi-colons to become a better writer.

- Include expanded noun phrases and description.

- Use formal language.

- Sub-headings.

Rainbow Newt

Within the South region of America, the Rainbow Newt has been discovered in the midst of the Tongas's forest. The Rainbow Newt is an extremely rare lizard as only one has been uncovered; many more will continue to haunt the remains of the spectacular forest of L.A. (Los Angeles).

What does the Rainbow Newt look like?

It reaches out to half a meter, and it has a tail as long as a slithering snake. Its pitch-black, bulging, beady, button eyes are utterly hypnotising, with a distinctive rainbow-patterned back. However, its quick hands are webbed between each individual digit, allowing it to rapidly sprint across the tiny ponds.

Diet

The Rainbow Newt is in fact a herbivore – meaning its entire diet is based of plants. Although they tend to prefer to eat shrubs which are dumped and moist like glossy green crunchy leaves; luscious luminous petals; soggy, wet, damp moss balls; and flavoursome crispy stems.

Did you know?

The appealing lovely lizard can camouflage large in many different circumstances. It is an inch away from extinction due to the fact it's at the bottom of its food chain and has MANY unwanted predators such as eagles and hawks.

Script

My tips:

- Use a colon after the character's name or in a list.

- Stick to three scenes, four maximum, as they take a long time to write.

- Try make it as enthralling as possible so the reader isn't bored.

- Include background noises here and there.

- You don't need speech marks.

Hogwarts is here!

Act 1:

Scene 1:

Curtains open, Harry Potter, who has jet-black hair and hazel brown eyes, is cautiously clinging onto the shiny, silver shopping basket. The basket has: spell books, a snow owl (Hedwig), wand and spare school clothes. In a state of confusion, Harry watches another boy – who is the same age as him – rapidly run through a brick-red wall.

Harry	: (Mumbles to himself.) Umm… So, I should be at platform 9-3/4? (Looks forward after staring at the train ticket.) Wait what! There's only a brick wall!
Hedwig	: (Staring with his beady eyes at Harry in complete bafflement). Hoo! Hoo!
A boy Harry's age	: Ekk… Gosh I'm so excited; can we go in together, mum?
Boy's mum	: Sure, okay let me countdown. Three…Two… One! (Runs with son through the wall.)
Background noise	: Poof!
Harry	: Wow they disappeared! I guess it's my go. What if I smash into the wall? Never mind. (Harry charges forward.)

Backroom noise : Poof, Harry is gone.

Curtains shut.

End of scene one.

Scene 2:

Curtains open, Harry boards the train and meets the boy he saw at the platform.

Harry : My name's Harry. What's your name?

The boy : Yup, my name is Ron. Ron Weasley. Are you, Harry, as in Harry Potter?

Harry : Yep, that's me. (Pushes his fringe away to reveal the 'z' shaped scar.)

Ron : WICKED! I wish I had a cool scar too. Anyways, let's go to get drinks and some candy. (Gets up and walks to the back of the Hogwarts Express.)

Harry : Okay. (Follows Ron.)

Ron : (Annoyed because a boy is not moving to let him pass.) You, fat elephant, move up!

Everyone chuckled apart from Harry.

The boy : Or what?

Ron : (Bravely) Oh, my fist will be in your face so it's as flat as the pancake I had for breakfast. See, but I ate it, and I can't eat you, can I?

Everyone but Harry roared with laughter.

Harry was appalled by Ron's, outrageous behaviour and walked off to sit with a different kid.

Curtains close.

End of scene two.

Scene 3:

Curtains open. They arrive at Hogwarts! The doors open and everyone pushed and shoved each other to get to the front to see the amazing Hogwarts.

A boy : Move! (Pushing his way through, to the doors of the train).

A girl : You move, you're the one blocking the way!

Harry on the other hand manages to squeeze past everyone and gets out.

Harry : Wow! (Gasping as he fixates his eye on Hogwarts school which looks like a giant castle.)

Teacher : Welcome students, to Hogwarts, school for young fellow witches and wizards. This will be your new home, and we are pleased to have all of you.

Background noise: everyone claps.

Teacher : Follow me to the castle so that you can settle in. (Walks to the stone castle as everyone follows nervously.)

Writing Examples

Glossary

Cascaded	– Something that flows down
Circumstances	– a fact that changes the situation
Controversial	– causing an argument/ dispute
Deficiency	– When you don't have enough of
Delectable	– Tasting or looking very nice
Discrimination	– Treating a group of people differently
Distinctive	– Easy to spot or recognise
Essential	– Very important or necessary
Fixated	– Unable to stop thinking about someone or something.
Fluctuate	– Change continuously on a graph
Incessantly	– Continuous without stopping
Intricate	– Incredibly detailed/ complicated
Inquisitive	– Wanting to learn/ discover something as much as possible in a way that annoys others.
Miscellaneous	– random things that aren't connected
Obesity	– Being dangerously fat

Oblivious	– Not conscious of your surrounding
Ominous	– Suggesting that something bad is going to happen.
Potentially	– Possible
Precautions	– an action done to prevent something
Resplendent	– Beautiful appearance
Restrictions	– A limit on something
Scintillating	– Shining and sparkly
Substantial	– A lot of value or importance
Succulent	– A piece of food which is nice and juicy.
Transpired	– Be revealed or come to be known
Vulnerable	– Able to easily get hurt mentally or physically.

Milton Keynes UK
Ingram Content Group UK Ltd.
UKHW020805311023
431661UK00015B/743